THE IMAGINARY WORLD OF

_____

YOUR NAME HERE ↗

KERI SMITH

PENGUIN BOOKS

PENGUIN BOOKS

An imprint of Penguin Random House LLC
375 Hudson Street
New York, New York 10014
penguin.com

First published in the United States of America by Perigee,
an imprint of Penguin Group (USA) LLC, 2014
Published in Penguin Books 2016

ISBN: 978-0-399-16525-2

PRINTED IN THE UNITED STATES OF AMERICA

10

Art and design by Keri Smith

ALL GROWN-UPS WERE ONCE CHILDREN...
BUT ONLY FEW OF THEM REMEMBER IT.
—ANTOINE DE SAINT-EXUPÉRY

TO TILDEN AND IDA,
MAY YOU ALWAYS REMEMBER.

CONTENTS

WHERE YOU CAN SEE THE FUN THINGS YOU ARE GOING TO DO

Introduction vi

A Few Words About Utopia by Steve Lambert ix

How to Use This Book x

Imaginary World Toolkit xi

    —*Tips and Visualization Techniques* xi

    —*Thought Experiments* xiii

    —*The Mooreeffoc Effect* xiv

The Database xvi

Begin 1

You Are About to Enter… 2

Describe the Street 5

Plan a Landscape 8

Describe the Weather 11

Create Your Home 13

Start a Map 14

Choose Your Persona 19

Write Your Imaginary Bio 21

List Your Secret Identities 22

Create the Characters 25

Give Life to Your Characters 26

Name Your World 29

Design Your World's Center/Headquarters 31

Create Your Own Currency 32

Conjure Magical Powers 35

Create the Invisible 37

Teach a Class 39

Write Some Books 41

Create a Special Place for Yourself 43

Here Are Some Mountains 45

How to Write a Manifesto 46

Create a Manifesto 47

Make a Rules of Conduct and Constitution 48

Build a Museum 51

Design a Logo/Symbol 53

Create a Wardrobe 55

Devise a Menu 57

Write a List of Secret Dreams 58

Here Is a Shop 61

Begin a Fictitious History 63

Create Historical Artifacts 65

Create Some New Inventions and Devices 67

Describe an Imaginary Adventure 69

Describe Your Transportation 71

Here Is a Tree 72

Create a Dictionary 74

Design a Poster 77

Create a New Holiday 78

Plan for Future Expansion 80

Build a Secret Laboratory 83

Add Portraits of Notable Inhabitants 85

Plan a Parade 87

Add Images or Photos 88

Create a Gathering Space 91

Create a Space Based on a Memory 93

Add a Park 95

Walk at Night 97

Describe the Businesses in Your World 99

Base Part of Your World on Your Favorite Novel or Film 101

Write a Traveler's Guide 103

Create a Soundtrack 105

Create an Area That Is Conceptual 106

Transform Parts of the Real World 109

Add an Unexplored Territory 111

Form an Organization in Your World 113

Make a Map of Your Day 115

Reference Your World 117

Create a Section of Your World That Is Used Solely for Play 119

Create an Area Based on Something You Love to Do 121

Create a Time Capsule 123

Document the Plant Life 125

Describe the Different Species 127

Here Is an Island 129

Build a Shrine or Monument 131

Create a Structure out of Your Favorite Material 133

Additional Tools 135

Brainstorming Methods 136

Tips for Beginners 137

Randomizing Function 138

Idea Generator 141

How to Make a Floorplan 142

Map Items 145

Device Parts 147

Structures 149

Certificate of Citizenship 151

What to Do with Your World 152

How to Work with Cardboard 153

List of Variables 154

Research Other Imaginary Worlds 157

Notes 159

INTRODUCTION

<u>THE THREE SECRETS</u>
<u>OF MAGIC</u>
(THE DISTILLATION
OF CENTURIES OF
HERMETIC KNOWLEDGE)

1. REALITY IS NOT
ALWAYS WHAT IT
SEEMS TO BE.

2. IMAGINATION
CREATES REALITY.

3. REALITY IS MADE
UP OF WORDS.*

— FERDINANDO BUSCEMA
(MAGICIAN)

* AND IMAGES. (AUTHOR'S
ADDITION FOR THE PURPOSE
OF THIS BOOK.)

The act of creating a world is an act of revolution.

To imagine something different, something better, or something more interesting is to push the existing world into a state of change. Some of the greatest revolutionary acts of our time came to be because someone had the courage to imagine something new.

If it is true that imagination creates our reality, then we can view ourselves as alchemists, able to transform society and the culture at large with our words and ideas. We have the power to heal an ailing culture with the "magical energy" that comes from our imaginations. Just by documenting our ideas, we can begin the process of change.

It's time to begin.

Remember: You have immense powers!

This book begins with a list.

You will be asked to write down a detailed list of everything you are drawn to—things that you love, that fascinate you, that get you excited, that you like to look at, that you collect. Include objects, colors, sounds,

"We carry within us the wonders we seek without us." —Sir Thomas Browne

textures, smells, materials, food, memories, places, and people. Make the list as long as you can. This list will be called "the Database."

You will use the items in the Database as the building blocks for creation—the same way a painter uses paint—to create texture and to build a foundation for the place you will inhabit. Your imaginary world will be based entirely on who you are as an individual and as such will be completely unique.

Once you have finished the Database you can move on to complete the prompts. You will often be asked to refer back to the list for material to use when shaping the world.

Everyone dreams about where they would like to live, what they would like to do with their time, how things could be better than their current situation. Some dream of how the world could be better and what that would look like. Others dream of completely new ways of running society, alternative political systems, new economies. In the pages of this book, you have permission to create your own reality.

WHAT KIND OF WORLD WOULD YOU LIKE TO INHABIT?

"Reality is always refracted through the imagination, and it is through our imagination that we live our lives." —Steven Duncombe

You probably already have some ideas tucked away from when you were little (when we allowed ourselves to create imaginary worlds all the time). Think back to your childhood: What activities did you most enjoy? What were you obsessed with when you were playing? If you were always riding your bike, maybe you created a story in your head about what you were doing, e.g., you were a world explorer on an important adventure. Draw on these ideas when creating your imaginary world.

As you create your world, know that it doesn't need to make sense in a literal way—let it evolve on its own. Maybe some parts are completely ridiculous and absurd, or strange and magical— this is good! Push your imagination to its furthest limits. Dabble as much as possible in the impossible—it can be much more interesting.

Your imaginary world can serve as the basis for all of your other future projects, (see **What to Do with Your World** on page 152). It can be the root of all that you will become and all that you will create in your life. Hopefully it will grow and change over time.

You now have unlimited powers of creation!

ALL AROUND US THE FUNDAMENTALS OF LIFE ARE CRYING OUT TO BE SHAPED, OR CREATED.
—JOSEPH BEUYS

(FROM A 1960S INTERVIEW WITH FRANS HAK.)

In creating an imaginary world, what we are really attempting is to define our idea of utopia, a reimagining of a world we would like to live in. To further explain the concept of utopia, I consulted Steve Lambert, artist and codirector of the Center for Artistic Activism, an organization committed to strengthening connections between social activism and artistic practice.

A FEW WORDS ABOUT UTOPIA
BY STEVE LAMBERT

The problem with reality is **it's so easy to see.**

Look around. There it is.

Go outside. There's some more.

You can't leave reality's presence. It's always there to remind you and it all seems so tangible and permanent. So real.

In fact, it's not permanent at all. Things are always changing, and in the long term, everything is temporary. Also, our idea of what reality is is never complete—after all, we can't know everything. On top of that, our idea of reality is usually inaccurate—some of the great moments in life are when we learn things and change our minds. That's how we grow.

When we think about the future, this reality can get in the way. Our incomplete and incorrect ideas of reality, and reality's persistence, end up tainting our imagination of what is probable in the world. The resulting visions of the future are tainted as well, and usually not very different from our current sense of reality.

It takes extra effort and imagination to set those tainted visions aside and dream up a reality we'd prefer, not to mention explore the innumerable futures that are possible.

But why do this? It is certainly more difficult.

Well, it's more fun. The world as it is could be a lot better. If you're going to imagine the future, it's a lot more joyful when you can escape from mistakes we've already made and envision something radically new. But there is another reason.

Utopia is a combination of three Greek words: Eu (good), Ou (not), and Topos (place). Utopia translated means "good not place." It is important to remember, as a "not place," that it is impossible to arrive at utopia. The reason we imagine utopias is to provide a point on the compass that orients us on our travels. Without utopia, we're lost—we are traveling without direction, guessing and hoping that we are moving forward. The purpose of utopia is not a destination, it is to give us direction so we can progress.

HOW TO USE THIS BOOK

(1) Choose the documenting format that works best for you (writing, drawing, collage, or a combination).

(2) The beginning prompts are designed as a warm-up, but feel free to skip around. Go directly to sections that make you the most excited.

(3) All prompts are open to interpretation. They exist to help spur your imagination but are not required.

(4) Feel free to change or ignore prompts that don't speak to you. Use only what works for your world and your personality; for example, you may not want to create a manifesto, you may prefer to create characters.

(5) If you become obsessed with or really enjoy a certain part of world creation, focus your energy on that. It may lead you to an interesting place.

(6) You may wish to break out of the space in the book and move to a larger area. Find some cardboard, or tape sheets of paper together.

(7) Use only what you have at your disposal. For example, visit the recycling box, look for wood in the garage, find bits of wool on an old sweater, repurpose an old shoebox.

IMAGINARY WORLD TOOLKIT

This section contains some methods to help you in your world creation. Pick and choose as you wish. Use what speaks to you!

TIPS AND VISUALIZATION TECHNIQUES

1. Take a walk in your neighborhood. Pay attention to things that pique your interest (e.g., trees, buildings). Use them as a basis for things in your world but alter them slightly. Turn them into magical items.

2. Take a long walk. At least an hour. Let your subconscious do some work for you. Ask it to brainstorm while you walk. Remain open and receptive but don't think too much about the ideas. Let them come in when they are ready. Do not judge the ideas when they come in. Just write them down (or draw them). Reserve time to take long walks on a regular basis.

3. Imagine alternatives to the life you are leading now. Where would you like to go/live/explore? What would you like to become? What gets you so excited you can't sleep at night? What do you see that no one else sees? What would you do if time/money/circumstance were no object? What makes you angry about your current world?

4. Take time away from technology. Give your mind a rest to allow for new ideas to surface.

5. Carry this book with you everywhere you go. Ideas will come up when you least expect them (often at night). Attach a pencil to the book so you can write them down immediately.

6. Your world can be alive and animated. You may wish to use things from this world (or other cultures in this world) to base your ideas upon. For example, the films of Hayal Miyazaki reflect Japan's Shinto belief system. An animistic religion, Shinto sees gods and spirits in everything, emphasizing harmony with the natural world. The spirits are visible to those who are open to seeing them (usually young children), and take a variety of forms; for example, soot balls are dust spirits that will dirty your home when you are not looking. What might a wood spirit look like? A river spirit? A paper spirit? Why would they visit you?

7. You are invited to make mock-ups of some of the things in your imaginary world. See page 153.

8. If you are having trouble starting from scratch, it helps to take an existing place that you are familiar with and use it as a base to start from. Draw a map of it and then you can alter the things in it to reflect your tastes and desires.

9. Have your favorite books with you when you are thinking of ideas. You have permission to BORROW and STEAL from them for inspiration in building your world. You do not have to copy the ideas directly, but take some of the ideas and alter them slightly.

10. Use the randomizing feature on page 138 to help you create objects, devices, and structures.

11. If you feel stuck, refer back to the Database, the source of all things that inspire you. Within that list you can find the spirit of the world you are creating. Start with the things you know very well and move on to the experimental.

12. Don't be afraid to try things. You don't have to like everything you do—just experiment to see what happens. You can always erase or revise the parts you don't like. You could try one type of structure for your home, and if it doesn't feel right, change it later into something else.

13. At the end of this book, there is a list of variables (potential things you could add to your world) that includes different types of buildings, climates, etc. You may use this to give you ideas for what to add. You could also choose things randomly from the list, if you like.

THOUGHT EXPERIMENTS

THE RIDDLE
DOES NOT
EXIST.
IF A QUESTION
CAN BE PUT
AT ALL, THEN
IT CAN ALSO
BE ANSWERED.

—LUDWIG
WITTGENSTEIN

Some of the best ideas can come from playing with thought experiments. This is when the act of posing a question and then answering it gives you a whole range of ideas that you might not have thought of. The question might take you down roads you never expected.

You can use thought experiments when creating your imaginary world. They can be particularly helpful if you're stuck for ideas. For example: What if the characters in your world had to build their own houses using only what they could find? What would they look like?

Here are some other questions you might like to try:

What if the characters in your world could only see certain colors? How would that affect their whole world?
What if certain objects were very small? Very large?
What if the only pigment found in your world was blue?
What if your world was vertical?
What if some buildings were made of ice?
What if your world was floating? Suspended?
What if some of the everyday objects were magic?
What if you could wear your house?

THE MOOR**ƎƎ**ᖴᖴ**OƆ** EFFECT

The Mooreeffoc Effect is about taking something that you are familiar with and essentially holding an imaginary mirror up to it to change your perspective—taking the familiar and shifting it just slightly to make it appear unfamiliar and strange. The term was created by Charles Dickens when he entered a coffee shop one day and noticed that the words "Coffee Room" were reversed on the window when you were standing inside. This had the effect of transforming a familiar space into something new and strange: a place with a language he did not understand.

MOOREEFFOC DEFINITION

"coffee-room, viewed from the inside through a glass door, as it was seen by Dickens on a dark London day" . . . used by Chesterton to denote the queerness of things that have become trite, when they are seen suddenly from a new angle." —J.R.R. Tolkien

(You can experience this by taking a familiar word and writing it out over and over until you don't recognize it anymore and it becomes nonsense.)

We can use this technique in creating our imaginary worlds by taking places and spaces we are very familiar with and altering them just slightly, adding something unexpected or strange. Think about adding something mysterious or puzzling to a scene. What if there was a tiny door in the bottom of your favorite tree? What if a page in one of your books was in code? What if the kitchen in your home had a trapdoor that no one had noticed before? Where does it lead? What if a mirror reflected a different scene than what was expected? You might also want to try creating anagrams out of familiar place names to come up with some new place names for your world. An anagram is a word formed by rearranging the letters of another word.

THE DATABASE

"Don't bend; don't water it down; don't try to make it logical; don't edit your own soul according to the fashion. Rather, follow your most intense obsessions mercilessly."
—Franz Kafka

These few pages will become the building blocks of your world. You will refer to them often, so you may choose to mark them in a way so you can find them easily.

WHAT KIND OF WORLD WOULD YOU LIKE TO INHABIT?

What kind of world would you like to retreat to?

List some things that you like and dislike about the current world.

List things that you like and dislike from different eras in history, if any come to mind.

What invokes wonder in you? Include everything that you are fascinated by.

CATEGORIES

Write down the things you love in each category. If you need more space, use the back notes section.

Books
Movies
Music
Colors
Materials/Textures
Smells
Sounds
Landscape
Climate/Weather

Time Periods/Eras
Places/Spaces
Animals
Artists
Clothing
People
Objects
Play/Toys/Entertainment

A BRIEF PERSONAL HISTORY

(Where are you from? Where is your family from?)

List things from your history that you respond to and that make you unique (stories, crafts, memories, characters, etc.)

MATERIALS

Collect and create a page of textures.

IMAGES

Collect images of things that fill you with wonder/excitement (use a journal, Pinterest, etc.).

List any personality traits about yourself that you feel are unique or different.

Add anything else you would like to have on your list of things that inspire you.

AUTHOR'S NOTE:

I am going to assume if you are using this book that you would like a bit of help in beginning/creating your imaginary world. So forgive me for imposing some ideas for your world, they may not speak to the world you are trying to create. Some are borrowed from other imaginary worlds, some are from my own. Think of the beginning exercises as a warm up, a leaping off point if you will. They will give you a chance to see what areas you would like to develop further, and what parts you become obsessed with.

BEGIN

"Nothing happens unless first a dream." —Carl Sandburg

YOU ARE ABOUT TO ENTER...

one of the most amazing places imaginable. It is a place where anything can happen, anything you desire. And it is a place where great things are built. We must begin by conjuring up ideas from the deepest depths of your imagination. These ideas are already there, just waiting for you to access them. They've probably been there since you were very young. Maybe you have forgotten about them. Don't worry, all it takes is a little coaxing to remember again. Relax. Find a comfortable sitting position. Take several deep breaths. Remove all distractions, turn off all devices. Let all thoughts fade from your mind. Have a pen or pencil ready.

You are going to begin in one small corner of your world. From this tiny beginning, great things will grow. Think of a space or place that you really love. It may be a place you've been or it could be something you've seen a photo of. It should be a place that moves you more than most places; you should feel a bit giddy when you think about it. You will know it's a good one if you think about it

now and you feel a little burst of energy.

Place yourself there. Stand in front of it. Is it a structure? Is it a place in nature? Describe what you are looking at. Go closer. If it's a structure, what materials is it constructed with? What can you smell? What sounds do you hear? Enter the space. As you walk, look at all of the details, look closely. Closer. How do you feel? What do you like to do there?

Know that your experience of the place is unique; it speaks to you because it somehow embodies a part of who you are. Does the place have a name? If not, give it one. It is now yours.

Do something else to personalize the space—add a decoration (a photo, some flowers, a sign with the name, a collection of something you love), or something you use (some books, a piece of furniture, an article of clothing). If you need ideas for what to add, consult the Database.

Describe the place here.

This is how space begins, with words only, signs traced on the blank page.
—Georges Perec

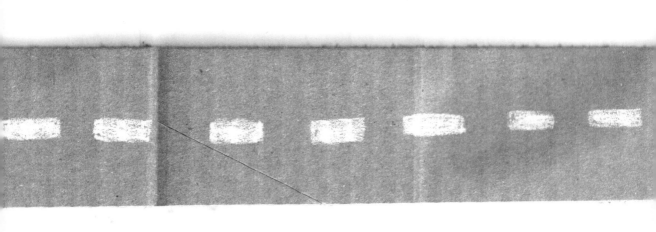

4

Now, leave this space and step outside. What is outside of this place? Maybe it is a street.

DESCRIBE THE STREET

It might help to first describe a street in your memory, one that you enjoy spending time on. Give the street a name.

Walk a few feet down the street. On your right-hand side there is what appears to be a mailbox. You see an envelope peeking out. You pull it out slightly and are surprised to find it is addressed to you. You open it. It reads:

THE NATIONAL CENTER FOR SPACE CREATION

You are receiving an award from the National Center for Space Creation for your amazing work in creating

_____

(name of your space here).

Congratulations! This is a big honor. In an effort to continue your vision, we are giving you funding to create some more spaces in the locations of your choice.

If you like what you've created, consider these the first additions to your world. Add their locations to the map on page 14.

If you don't, feel free to ditch it and start again with the following prompts.

YOU WILL NOW
PROCEED TO
BUILD THE
REST OF YOUR
WORLD PIECE
BY PIECE.

PLAN A LANDSCAPE

Pull out a few of the books from your list. Start thinking about what kinds of landscape(s) your imaginary world will be set in. (Some ideas to get you started: island, neighborhood, country, miniature world, floating world, desert, forest, outer space, subterranean, underwater, interplanetary, etc.) Feel free to include many different kinds of landscapes.

10

A CHANGE IN THE WEATHER
IS SUFFICIENT TO RECREATE
THE WORLD AND OURSELVES.
—MARCEL PROUST

DESCRIBE THE
WEATHER

What is the climate like in your world? Are
there seasons?

Granted there is a
wall, what's going on
behind it?
—Jean Tardieu

CREATE YOUR HOME

Describe your living space in detail. What kind of materials is it made from? Where is it located? Base it on a space where you feel most comfortable in the real world. Think of all the possibilities. What is your favorite space you've ever seen? Decorate it according to your taste. Some ideas: Maybe you are nomadic and the structure is impermanent, it could be a tree house, a boat, a castle. Incorporate a playful aspect. Draw a floor plan (see page 142 for tips).

START A MAP

Everything links back to and is connected by the map of your imaginary world. Draw your own version beginning on the next page as you work through the prompts. Start with your first building/location. You will add and change things as you go through the book. You can also cut out and use the pieces on the **Map Items** on page 145 to create your world. Include the locations you've visited so far, and all landmarks and places of interest. Just doodle, don't worry about making it look good. You can also make a collaged map using bits of cut-up paper. Here are some symbols to get you started, but you can make up your own too.

If you need more space, you can tape more pages to it, or get some large pieces of cardboard to draw it on. If you want, you can base it on a map of your current neighborhood and add/alter it as you wish.

"Every map is a guide to finding the desirable and navigating the dangerous."
—Rebecca Solnit, Infinite City

"A map does not just chart, it unlocks and formulates meaning; it forms bridges between here and there, between disparate ideas that we did not know were previously connected."
—Reif Larsen, The Selected Works of T. S. Spivet

MAP SYMBOLS

- - - - - BOUNDARY	═══ ROAD	┼┼┼┼┼┼┼ RAILROAD	▬▬▬ BRIDGE
····· DIRT ROAD	WATER	TREES	☐ BUILDING
MOUNTAINS	GARDEN	PASTURE	MEADOW

ADD YOUR OWN

FURTHER RESEARCH: DIY CARTOGRAPHY

CHOOSE YOUR PERSONA

Who are you in this world? Who is your alter ego? What do you actually do in your world? List things you like to do: hobbies, obsessions, etc. If you do not wish to include yourself in your world, skip to page 25.

"You should never hesitate to trade your cow for a handful of magic beans." — Tom Robbins

WRITE YOUR IMAGINARY BIO

Include everything you would like to do as if it has already happened. If you have ever dreamed of doing something big, now is the time. List your credentials, skills, awards, accomplishments. Take on the qualities of your favorite people. You can choose to do this with imagery if you wish. Find images of things that represent what you would like to accomplish.

21

LIST YOUR SECRET IDENTITIES

Maybe you would like to try different professions/personalities. Change as you wish.

23

CREATE THE CHARACTERS

that live in your world. Are they human, animal, or something else? Where do they live? What do they do? What are their names? These characters can be imaginary or maybe you want to invite real people you admire to live there. Think of your favorite characters from books. What qualities did they have? You may borrow some traits from them. What excites them? When are they most active? Are they social or introverted? Are there inanimate objects that come alive when you are not looking?

GIVE LIFE TO YOUR CHARACTERS

Make a list of their daily activities. What places do they visit? What do they dream of? What kinds of objects do people make in your world? What tools do they use? What materials do they use? What are the objects used for? How do they survive and provide for themselves? Consult the Database for ideas based on your own interests.

27

"Our imagination flies—we are its shadow on the earth." —Vladimir Nabokov

NAME YOUR WORLD

Think about your favorite movies and books in the Database and mine them for ideas. If you do not wish to commit to a name during the building process, name it something general like Land of the Unknown.

DESIGN YOUR
WORLD'S CENTER/
HEADQUARTERS

What kind of space do you envision for it? Is it fun and playful, or serious and imposing? Is it permanent or temporary (nomadic)? Research different kinds of structures or vessels to get a sense of how they are constructed.

CREATE YOUR OWN CURRENCY

You now have as much money as you need. What do you do with it?

Currency can have imagery from various aspects of society, a notable figure (politicians, royalty, civil rights leaders, authors, etc.), an example of the nature in a region (leaves, animals, flowers), or a cultural event (sporting events, crafts, etc.). What would you put on yours?

Create your own economy. Research alternative economies for some ideas on how to form your own economic system. Can you come up with some new ways of sustaining your world?

"Everything you can imagine is real." —Pablo Picasso

CONJURE MAGICAL POWERS

(or assign some to your characters). Choose from this list: levitation, ESP, invisibility, etc. What do you/they use them for?

CREATE THE INVISIBLE

What can't you see in your world? Certain characters? Spaces?

37

TEACH A CLASS

What is it about? What are some skills you would like to share with others in order to affect your world? Write the curriculum. If you could create your own school, what would it be?

WRITE SOME BOOKS

List the books you have written in your imaginary world. What are they about? How are they distributed? Who is reading them?

CREATE A SPECIAL PLACE FOR YOURSELF

A secret spot you go to when you want to be alone. Describe the space. Is it tranquil or animated? Dark or bright? Perhaps it has some kind of landmark, such as a structure, a rock, a special tree, or a body of water. Give this spot a name. When do you go there? What do you like to do there? Add it to the map.

HERE ARE SOME MOUNTAINS

Who lives on these mountains? What is the name of the mountain range? Draw on them and add their location to your map.

HOW TO WRITE A MANIFESTO

A manifesto is a document you write that declares your goals, plans, and dreams. It is usually one page with bullet points (or in point form). Your manifesto will be read over and over again (to remind you what you are striving for and to keep you on track with your vision).

Write about what you are passionate about. What do you stand for? What are your beliefs?
What gifts and ideas do you have to share with the world?
What big dreams do you have for your life/group/organization? What would you like to accomplish? These can be serious goals, or they can be absurd (it's up to you).
Formulate a plan. Have some thoughts about how you might go about achieving these goals.
Research other manifestos and use some of the ideas you like.
Points can be as simple or complex as you like.
You may also add a list of dos and don'ts for you manifesto.

CREATE A MANIFESTO

What ideas, thoughts, or philosophies rule your world?

MAKE A RULES OF CONDUCT AND CONSTITUTION

List your ideas for creating a peaceful existence, as well as laws and principles that define the nature, functions, and limits of your world.

WE THE CITIZENS OF

_____

BUILD A MUSEUM

What would a museum in your world contain? Is it large or small? Is its location a secret or public? Use the items from the Database for ideas for contents. Maybe it is portable and moves around in some kind of vehicle. Or maybe it is underground.

"We're making it up. The world, the universe, life, reality. Especially reality." —Tom Robbins

DESIGN A LOGO/ SYMBOL

Make a flag or a badge using the symbol. Look at your Database for ideas for symbols. You might like to use a favorite animal, something from nature, a tool you like to use, or a drawing of a citizen. You can put this logo on any of the materials you create for your imaginary world.

CREATE A WARDROBE

What do you wear every day in your world? Do you make your own clothes? Do you have a bag of some kind? What do you carry in it? What tools do you have? Include all the things you will need to explore your world during all the seasons.

DEVISE A MENU

What kinds of foods can be found in your world? What foods do you eat? Place recipes here.

WRITE A LIST

58

OF SECRET DREAMS

Turn them into reality in your world.

HERE IS A SHOP

to add to your world. What kind of characters own this shop? What do they sell? Maybe it is something not available in our world. Maybe it is something that only certain people can see. Customize it (draw on it) and add it to your map.

BEGIN A FICTITIOUS HISTORY

Base it on a period of history that you respond to. Add a timeline. Alternate: Make up a creation myth for your world. How did it come to be? Did someone find it? Research creation myths from cultures other than your own.

CREATE HISTORICAL ARTIFACTS

Find some old things that you think are interesting (take a photo of them or draw them) and create a fictitious history for how they came to exist in your world. Some examples might be a uniform, a tool, a vessel (bowl or cup), or a piece of furniture.

CREATE SOME NEW

INVENTIONS

AND DEVICES

for your world. For some help with this you might like to use the **Idea Generator** on page 141, and **Device Parts** on page 147.

"When you see someone putting on his Big Boots, you can be pretty sure that an Adventure is going to happen." —A. A. Milne (Winnie-the-Pooh)

DESCRIBE AN IMAGINARY ADVENTURE

that you or your characters go on in your world. What places would you like to visit/explore? Do you need some kind of vehicle or vessel for the adventure? What do you find?

WHY, SOMETIMES I'VE BELIEVED
AS MANY AS SIX IMPOSSIBLE THINGS
BEFORE BREAKFAST.
—LEWIS CARROLL

DESCRIBE YOUR TRANSPORTATION

What kind of transportation do you use in your imaginary world? Describe it in detail. How does it work? Does it require power of some kind?

HERE IS A TREE

to add to your world. What if a whole world was going on inside this tree? Draw what you think might be happening inside. Or add something to the outside. Does this tree have a special purpose?

73

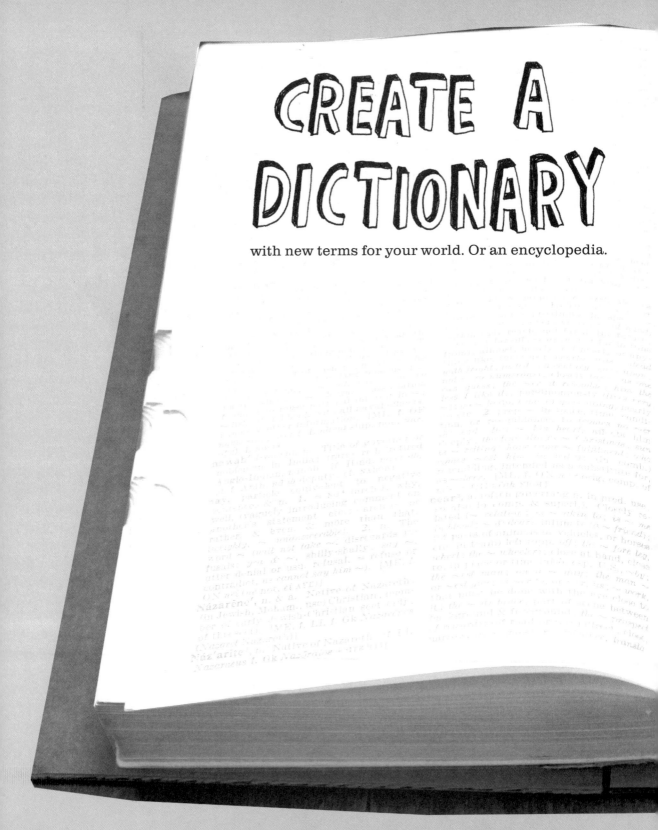

CREATE A DICTIONARY

with new terms for your world. Or an encyclopedia.

DESIGN A POSTER

INVITING PEOPLE TO VISIT YOUR IMAGINARY WORLD

You can offer certificates of citizenship
if you wish. Template on page 151.

CREATE A NEW

HOLIDAY

for your world based on something from your Database.

PLAN FOR FUTURE EXPANSION

If you wish to grow your world, how do you see it unfolding? How do you manage the resources? Can you brainstorm new ideas to make your world sustainable?

"If I had a world of my own, everything would be nonsense. Nothing would be what it is, because everything would be what it isn't. And contrariwise, what it is it wouldn't be. And what it wouldn't be, it would." —Lewis Carroll

BUILD A SECRET LABORATORY

This is a place for you to conjure up new ideas for your world. You might also use it for data collection and experiments. Collect and label specimens and materials that might be found in your world. Add your lab to the map. Some other ideas: brainstorming lab, research lab, meeting place for citizens, etc.

Microscopic Pleides

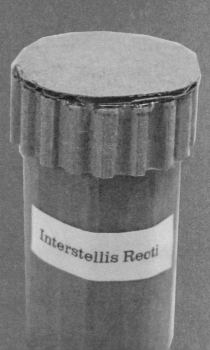

Interstellis Recti

ADD PORTRAITS OF NOTABLE INHABITANTS

You may use existing photos or draw and write notes about the citizens of your world.

PLAN A PARADE

What are people celebrating?
What is the theme? How are
the people dressed? Consult
the Database for ideas.

ADD IMAGES OR PHOTOS

THAT MIGHT COME FROM YOUR WORLD

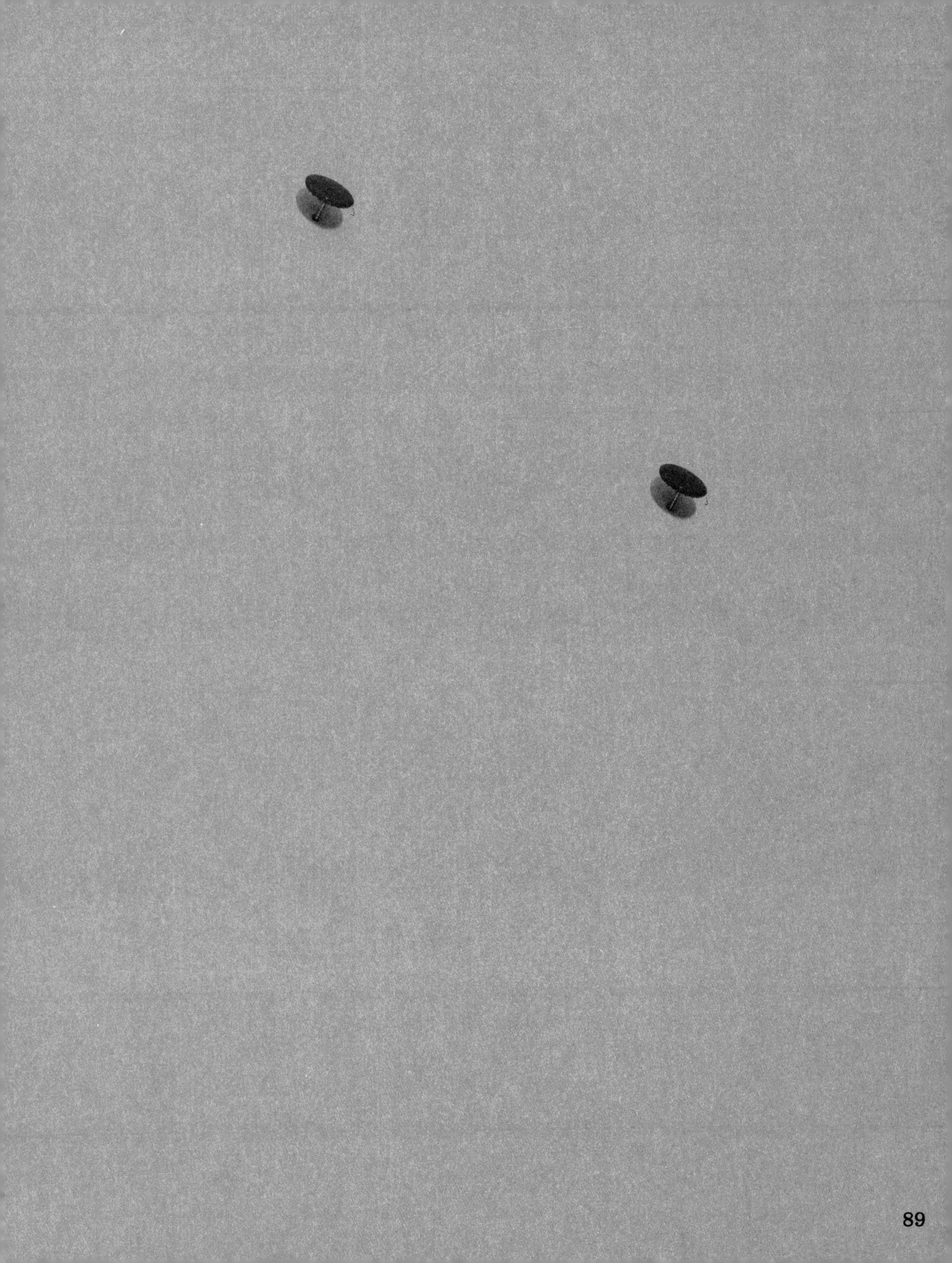

"Imagination is everything. It is the preview of life's coming attractions." —Albert Einstein

CREATE A GATHERING SPACE

for people who live in the world.

"What matters in life is not what happens to you but what you remember and how you remember it." —Gabriel García Márquez

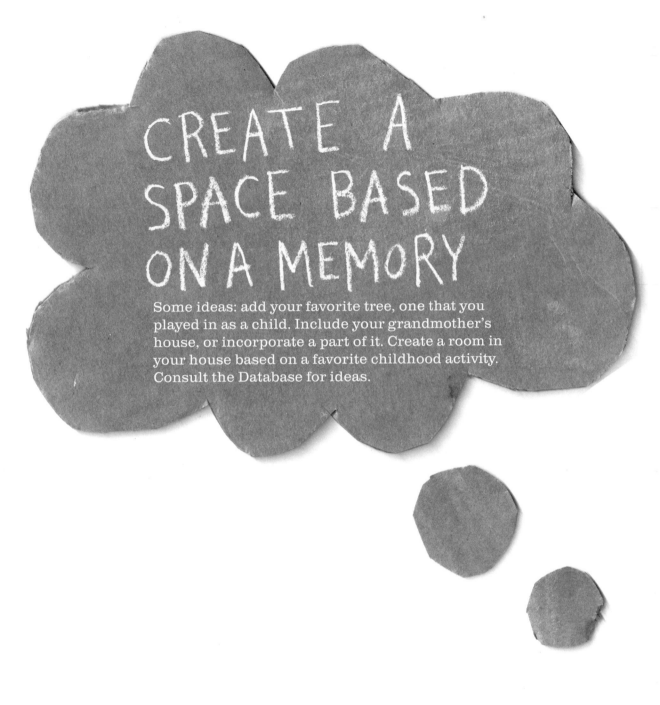

CREATE A SPACE BASED ON A MEMORY

Some ideas: add your favorite tree, one that you played in as a child. Include your grandmother's house, or incorporate a part of it. Create a room in your house based on a favorite childhood activity. Consult the Database for ideas.

ADD A PARK

inspired by something from your Database.

WALK AT NIGHT

What goes on in the darkness in your world? Write a list of nighttime happenings. What lurks in the shadows?

98

DESCRIBE THE BUSINESSES IN YOUR WORLD

What do they sell? How do you get to them? How do they contribute to the world? Add them to your map.

"Fiction is like a spider's web, attached ever so lightly perhaps, but still attached to life at all four corners." —Virginia Woolf

BASE PART OF YOUR WORLD ON YOUR FAVORITE NOVEL OR FILM

It doesn't have to be literal. Some ideas: create a shop that exists in a film, use a color theme from the book to create a space of some kind, invite characters from a book into your world, create a neighborhood based on one you've seen in a movie.

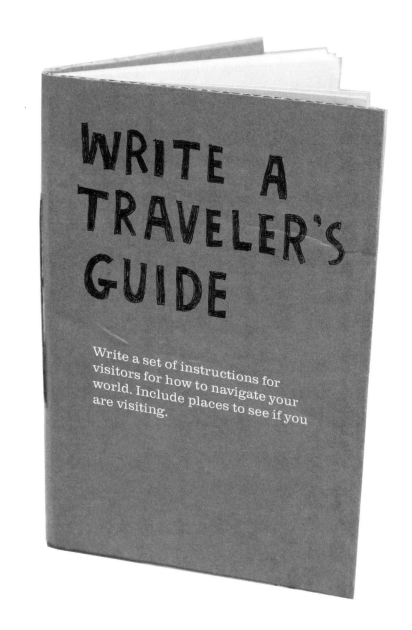

WRITE A TRAVELER'S GUIDE

Write a set of instructions for visitors for how to navigate your world. Include places to see if you are visiting.

103

CREATE A SOUND TRACK

for your world. What kind of music do you
think would go well as you move around
your environment? Choose something that
expresses the feel of your space.

CREATE AN AREA THAT IS CONCEPTUAL

(that is, based on one simple concept or idea).
Some ideas: an area where everyone gets lost, an
area based on one color, an area where everything
floats, an area where people go to dream.

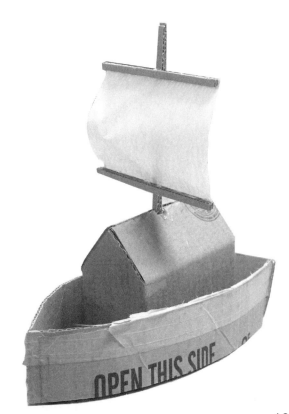

TRANSFORM PARTS OF THE REAL WORLD

Take a walk in your city or town.
Find some structures or buildings
that interest you, and take photos.
Incorporate the structures into your
imaginary world. Create a fictitious
history of the transformation.
Alternate: Think of something
you don't like in the real world.
Transform it into something better.

ADD AN UNEXPLORED TERRITORY

Is there a section of your world you have yet to explore? (Mark it as unexplored on the map.) What exists there? Is it scary? Is it mysterious?

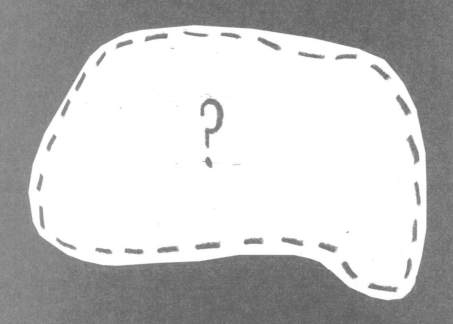

FORM AN ORGANIZATION
IN YOUR WORLD

It could be a political party, a secret club, etc. Come up with a name for it. Create its logo/symbol. What does it stand for? Add the location to the map.

MAKE A MAP OF YOUR DAY

that follows your or a character's activities in your world. What do you spend your time doing in this world?

REFERENCE YOUR WORLD

Write encyclopedic entries about all
the various parts of your world.

CREATE A SECTION OF YOUR WORLD THAT IS USED SOLELY FOR PLAY

What does that look like for you? A fort?
A suspended net? A treehouse?

CREATE AN AREA BASED ON SOMETHING YOU LOVE TO DO

(for example, if you like reading you could put reading nooks all throughout your world). Make a list of things you would keep in it. Add it to the map.

CREATE A TIME CAPSULE

based on your imaginary world. Include letters from inhabitants, photos of the world, drawings, sounds, tools, current technology used, etc. Consider what legacy you are leaving for future generations. What do these objects say about the current inhabitants?

DOCUMENT THE PLANT LIFE

Describe some of the plants and trees.

DESCRIBE THE DIFFERENT SPECIES OF ANIMALS

that make an appearance in your world.

128

HERE IS AN ISLAND

you might like to add to your world. Something strange is happening on this island. What is it? Draw on it and add it to your map.

BUILD A SHRINE OR MONUMENT

It should be based on something that is important to you, such as a person, a cause, something from history, a spiritual belief, or a ritual. What does it look like? Add it to the map.

CREATE A STRUCTURE

OUT OF YOUR FAVORITE MATERIAL

Some suggestions: tower, hut, bridge. Choose one of your favorite materials from the list. You will be creating a drawing of this structure, not making a physical version (unless you wish to). Determine the function of the structure. Work with the characteristics of the material. If your favorite material is wool, then it could be a knit structure. Brainstorm some different kinds of structures that are not common in our world, such as hanging or floating houses. Plan a spot for your structure in your world and add it to the map.

"The ability to 'fantasize' is the ability to survive. It's wonderful to speak about this subject because there have been so many wrong-headed people dealing with it....The so-called realists are trying to drive us insane, and I refuse to be driven insane....We survive by fantasizing. Take that away from us and the whole damned human race goes down the drain."

—Ray Bradbury

ADDITIONAL TOOLS

TOOLS

FOR WORLD CREATION

BRAINSTORMING METHODS

Brainstorming or Mind Mapping are very helpful when it comes to world creation. The secret is to capture ideas quickly, and get down as many of them as you can. The reason speed is helpful is that it doesn't give your inner critic time to second-guess things. Quantity is important because among the many ideas there will be a few that stand out for you—these are the ones that you must follow. One way to do this is to use spider charts, which connect ideas around a central subject. Your central subject in this case would be your imaginary world (put the name if you have one in the center of the page). You would then add some subtopics—these will be "branches" coming off of the center subject. These could be climate, wildlife, structures, organizations, inhabitants, literature, philosophy, transportation, history, devices, etc. You will then branch out on each topic, and even link topics if desired. If you prefer visual notes you can add small simple illustrations and color to your chart. Think about what problems you/we are currently facing in the real world. What would make them better? How could you incorporate playfulness?

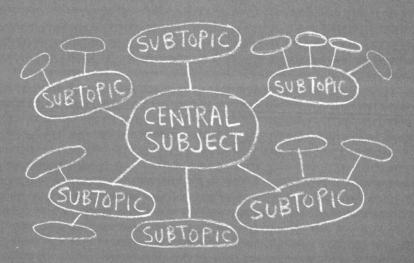

TIPS FOR BRAINSTORMING

WITHHOLD JUDGMENT

Do not censor your ideas. Write down the first things that come into your mind, even if you think they are not good.

QUANTITY OVER QUALITY

Write as many as you can. You can always scratch stuff out later.

WHAT WOULD _____ DO?

Insert your favorite author, filmmaker, illustrator, designer, teacher, etc.

GO CRAZY

Push yourself to go to places you've never been before. This is where the interesting stuff is. Are you dreaming of flying vessels and underground tunnels? Add them.

BUILD ON THE IDEAS OF OTHERS

Use concepts from your favorite books or movies. Alter them slightly. Change the scale. Make them bigger. Make them smaller. Change the colors. Change the names.

IF YOU GET STUCK TAKE A BREAK

Go do something else for a time and come back to it.

RANDOMIZING FUNCTION

If you have trouble deciding what to add you can use these cards to make the decision for you. It can also be interesting to build parts of your world using chance (e.g., picking out of a hat). Cut out the squares and put them in a hat or bowl. Pick one randomly and add the item to your world and the map. Add your own ideas to the blank squares, customize them to your own tastes.

FUN THINGS TO ADD

—hidden labyrinths, secret doors, tunnels, portals, furnished burrow, gardens, secret hideout, treehouse, slides, hanging structures, secret libraries, underwater laboratories, stairs, nooks, dark corners

—crazy vessels, vehicles, machines, bicycles

—robots, flying people, superheros, talking trees

—add more things from your database

river	desert	forest	farmland
island	park	village	library
airport	mountains	house	cave
ocean	yurt	post office	tunnel
character	restaurant	black hole	market

139

IDEA GENERATOR

Use this method for brainstorming new structures, vehicles, inventions, or devices.

DIRECTIONS

Make one list based on things you would like to add to your world. Structures (house, tipi, shop, yurt, bridge, beehive), vehicles (boat, bus, car, bike, airplane), or everyday devices (phone, bicycle, stereo).

Make a second list of different Materials (blocks, tubes, trees, ropes, wool). You could also make this a list of things found in nature if you prefer.

Make a third list of Action Verbs (flying, floating, moving, flashing, jumping, disappearing, sinking, blooming, growing, talking).

Combine one item from each list to come up with some new and interesting items. For example, a floating tipi made of tubes. If you don't like what you choose, try again.

HOW TO MAKE A FLOORPLAN

Your floorplan does not have to be to scale, you can just make it approximate. Start by drawing the basic shape, the outline of the structure. Use the legend below to add basic features. Create your own legend with some more interesting items!

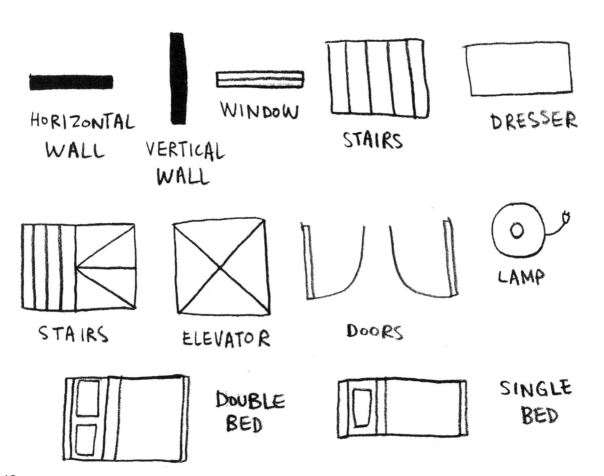

HORIZONTAL WALL

VERTICAL WALL

WINDOW

STAIRS

DRESSER

STAIRS

ELEVATOR

DOORS

LAMP

DOUBLE BED

SINGLE BED

COUCH

SIDE TABLE

COFFEE TABLE

REFRIGERATOR

RUG

CHAIR

CIRCULAR RUG

BATHTUB

WOOD STOVE

PLANT

BOOKSHELF

TOILET

TABLE

CHAIR

ROUND TABLE

SHOWER

SINK

DOUBLE SINK

STOVE

ROUND SINK

MAP ITEMS

Use these items for inspiration for your map. You can also cut them out and add them if you wish. Sometimes it helps to just start putting things down, add a few things and build from there. Start by defining the space a little.

MOUNTAINS

ROCKS

TOWER

VARIOUS SIZED STRUCTURES (TOP VIEW)

TREES

DIFFERENT HOUSE SHAPES

POND

IGLOO

TIPI

MUD HOUSE

CACTI

FENCE

BRIDGE

YURT

SPACE HOUSE

OLD FACTORY

MODERN BUILDING

TALL BUILDING

DEVICE PARTS

Use these parts to add a realistic touch to your devices (either drawings or three-dimensional versions). Add them to a regular cardboard box.

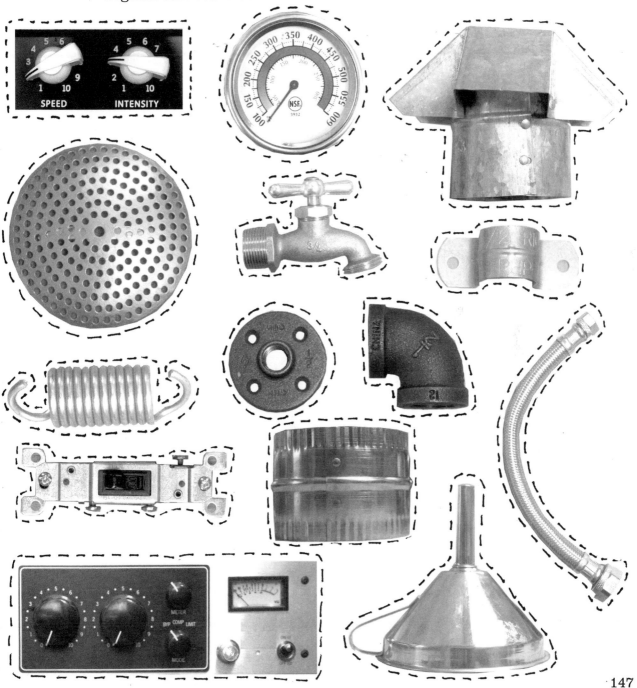

STRUCTURES

Here are some basic structures to embellish or brainstorm with.
Which feels most like you? What would turn them into "your" space?

CERTIFICATE OF CITIZENSHIP

Use this template to create a certificate of citizenship. What is the criteria for citizenship? Do you have any requirements? What do you ask citizens to contribute to your world? Add to it, make it yours. Often these kinds of documents will have a seal, which is a detailed logo to certify that the certificate is authentic. Use the logo you created for your world on your seal. Invite people to join.

NO. _____

CERTIFICATE OF CITIZENSHIP

This is to certify that

_____
(NEW CITIZEN SIGNATURE HERE.)

is an official citizen of

_____
(NAME OF WORLD)

DATED THIS _____ DAY OF _____ , ____ .

DATE OF BIRTH _____ .

SEX _____ . MARITAL STATUS_____ .

COUNTRY OF FORMER CITIZENSHIP_____ .

_____
SIGNATURE OF OFFICIAL

WHAT TO DO WITH YOUR WORLD

So now that you've created your imaginary world (or portions of it), you might be interested in taking it into another realm or using it as source material for another project.

List of things to use your imaginary world for: story, novel, screenplay, activism, artwork, sculpture, installation, songs, diorama, film, cartoons, comic book, video game, fields such as engineering, education, science, business, politics, etc.

Some activities to play with
—Create a sculpture based on some aspect of your world (i.e. create a structure that might exist in your world).
—Make a mock-up of your favorite outfit.
—Recreate your map in another medium (embroidery, painting, etc.).
—Make something that would exist in your world: a painting, a needlepoint, a costume, photos of residents (based on people you know in the real world), etc.
—Make a short film based in your world.

—Create an installation (or a website) displaying all of the things you have created for your world and describing it in detail. Create a piece of land art based on your world (research other examples of land art).
—Try collaborating with someone else; create a world together. Take turns adding things.
—Pretend your world is real when you go out. Play your soundtrack from page 105 on headphones—music makes the world seem more otherworldly. Look for places and objects that could be a part of your world, a special tree, a street, a statue.
—Create guerrilla art pieces based on your world and leave them out in public (some examples: an underground mail system with tiny mailboxes, your poster or flyer from page 77 inviting people to visit your world, a small portal that leads to your imaginary world).
—Create a small talisman (a charm, jewelry, card, T-shirt) from your world (include your symbol from page 53) to carry with you when you go out.
—Pretend you are a character from your world. Go on an adventure as that character (what would they do?).

HOW TO WORK WITH CARDBOARD

TO CREATE PARTS OF YOUR WORLD IN 3D!

YOU CAN MAKE ANYTHING OUT OF CARDBOARD AND IT'S ABUNDANT AND FREE!

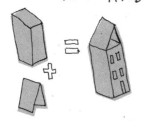

THE QUICK METHOD

Find boxes the size you want. Add to them to get your desired shape.

CUTTING MAT

CUTTING

Use scissors if the cardboard is thin and the shape is simple. A utility knife works best for corrugated cardboard. Preferably use with a cutting mat. Be very mindful of your fingers.

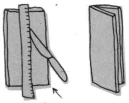

FOLDING

SCORING

Using a blunt object (butter knife, folding bone, ruler), score a folding line. Place a ruler where you would like the fold and run the knife down the ruler pressing firmly. Fold on the line.

ROLLING

Create bends parallel to the ridges in the cardboard.

LAMINATING

Glue several pieces of cardboard together to create a solid shape or to create a stronger material to build with.

Use a hot glue gun for the fastest and strongest method. Tape or glue along edges.

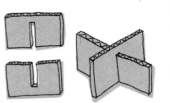

INTERLOCKING

This is a good method for making figures that stand or for creating something that can hold weight.

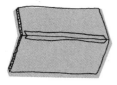

ASSEMBLING

LIST OF

USE THIS LIST TO GET YOU THINKING

MAKE YOUR OWN LIST

VARIABLES

THINGS TO EXPERIMENT WITH OR ADD

MOOD/ENERGY

SCALE

MICRO/MACRO

SHAPE

TEMPERAMENT

COLOR

STORY

TEXTURE

PHILOSOPHY

EDUCATION

VARIABLES

LAYOUT

POLITICS

CULTURE

SOCIETY

MOVEMENT

JUMPING
FLOATING
FLYING
SAILING
FALLING
SWINGING
DANCING
ZOOMING
FLIPPING
TIPPING
CREEPING
SINKING
SLINKING
SPEEDING

CLIMATE

TROPICAL
MID-LATITUDE
POLAR
MOIST
DRY

GEOGRAPHY

ICE/ARCTIC
DESERT
MOUNTAINS
OCEANIC

154

STRUCTURES

SHED
FARMHOUSE
GREENHOUSE
HAYLOFT
STABLE
WINDMILL
WATERMILL
MARKET
SILO
MARINA
BANK
CAFE
BAR
HOTEL
ARENA
MALL
SHOP
PUB
WAREHOUSE
HOUSE
APARTMENT
PORTAL
SPACE STATION
VILLA
FLYING HOUSE

BATH HOUSE
BARN
AIRPORT
BUNGALOW
CASTLE
YAODONG
CHALET
COTTAGE
DORMITORY
DOMUS
EARTH HOUSE
GUEST HOUSE
HOSPITAL
LOG CABIN
LONG HOUSE
MONASTERY
RIAD
PARLIAMENT
ROUND HOUSE
SOD HOUSE
TREE HOUSE
CAVE
TINY HOUSE
POST OFFICE

INN
HUT
BURROW
LIBRARY
CITY HALL
CONSULATE
COURTHOUSE
STATION
FORT
BEACH HUT
IGLOO
GALLERY
MUSEUM
CINEMA
FIRE STATION
POLICE STATION
CHURCH
TEMPLE
PAGODA
TRAIN STATION
CARAVAN
SCHOOL
COLLEGE
THEATER
MOSQUE
BRIDGE
WORKSHOP
BOAT
TENT
YURT
PANDAL
TIPI
LAVVU
KOHTE
GOAHTI

155

RESEARCH

OTHER IMAGINARY WORLDS

For the most extensive collection of imaginary worlds consult:

Dictionary of Imaginary Places by Alberto Manguel and Gianni Guadalupi

Some other people and places to explore:

The Book of Legendary Lands by Umberto Eco
Nowhere Island by Alex Hartley: nowhereisland.org
The House That Herman Built: hermanshouse.org
Jerry's Map: jerrysmap.blogspot.com
Andrea Zittel: zittel.org
Luigi Prina's flying boats
Winnie-the-Pooh by A. A. Milne
Charles Dellschau
Buckminster Fuller

All works of fiction

NOTES
SOME EXTRA SPACE TO WORK

NOTES

NOTES

NOTES

NOTES

KERI SMITH IS A SECRET AGENT AND WORLD EXPLORER LIVING IN A SMALL CABIN IN THE WOODS, ALLEGEDLY NOT FAR FROM THE VILLAGE OF ELFRENTOHS. SHE SPENDS HER DAYS WANDERING AND SEARCHING FOR FOREST SPIRITS, WHO OFTEN APPEAR IN THE FORM OF LARGE ROCKS AND CROOKED TREES (MOST OFTEN LEFT LEANING NOT RIGHT). ON OCCASION SHE ALSO FINDS A RIVER SPIRIT (THOUGH THEY ARE NOT NEARLY AS COMMON). WHEN SHE IS NOT INVOLVED IN EXPLORATIONS SHE SPENDS TIME CREATING NEW INVENTIONS DESIGNED TO HELP WITH TIME TRAVEL, ENLIGHTENMENT AND INVISIBILITY. SHE HAS RECENTLY BEEN WORKING ON BRAINSTORMING ALTERNATIVES TO THE CURRENT ECONOMIC SYSTEM, STOPPING CLIMATE CHANGE AND CONTEMPLATING THE FUTURE OF THE BOOK.

FOR MORE INFORMATION ON HER WORK PLEASE VISIT KERISMITH.COM

OPEN THIS SIDE

AVAILABLE FROM PENGUIN BOOKS

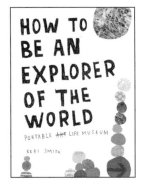

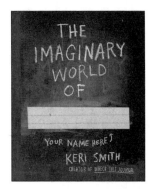

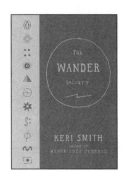

PENGUIN BOOKS